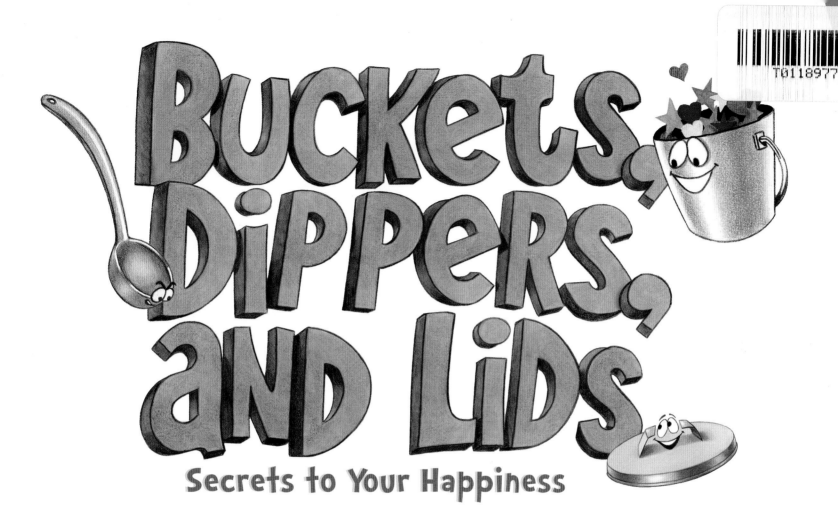

Buckets, Dippers, and Lids

Secrets to Your Happiness

By Carol McCloud · Illustrated by Glenn Zimmer

www.CardinalRulePress.com

Author's Acknowledgments

In the 1960s, Dr. Donald O. Clifton (1924-2003) first created the "Dipper and Bucket" story that has now been passed along for decades. Dr. Clifton later went on to co-author the #1 New York Times bestseller *How Full is Your Bucket?* and was named the Father of Strengths-based Psychology.

Illustrated by Glenn Zimmer
Redesigned by Maggie Villaume

Description: The concept of an invisible bucket and dipper encourages kind and considerate behavior, discourages poor behavior, and teaches the benefits of positive relationships.

Library of Congress Data

LCCN 2017950616 (print)
ISBN 9781945369018 (paperback)
ISBN 9781945369025 (hardcover)
ISBN 9781945369032, 9781945369049, 9780945369056,
   9781945369094 (ebooks)

Cardinal Rule Press

5449 Sylvia
Dearborn Heights, MI 48125
Visit us at www.CardinalRulePress.com

Before Reading

- Looking at the cover, can you guess the feelings of the soup ladle, the bucket and lid?

- Based on the cover and title, what do you think this story is about?

- Have you heard of "filling a bucket" before? If so, what do you know about it?

During Reading

- Has anyone ever dipped into your bucket?

- What are some ways you can practice putting a lid on your bucket?

- How can you fill your bucket at the same time you fill someone else's bucket?

After Reading

- How do the bucket, the dipper, and the lid all fit together?

- What do you think your bucket looks like?

- If you already knew about bucket filling, what is something new that you learned from this story?

Buckets

Dippers

Lids

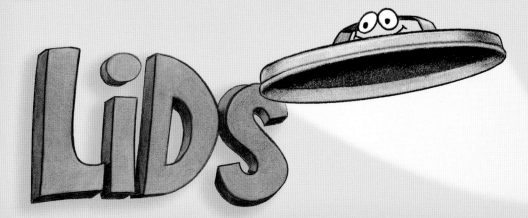

Do you know that everyone in the whole world has an invisible bucket, an invisible dipper, and an invisible lid?

It's true. EVERYONE!
Whatever your age, wherever you live,
whatever you look like on the outside,
you have an invisible bucket, dipper, and lid.

Knowing how buckets, dippers, and lids work will help you learn
three secrets to your happiness.

Your bucket belongs to only you.

It has been with you since the day you were born.

Your bucket is not an ordinary bucket that holds water or sand.

It's where you hold all your happiness.

When you were little, you depended on other people to fill your bucket.

They filled your bucket when they held you, played with you, and took good care of you. They also filled your bucket when they changed your stinky diapers.

As you grew, you started
to fill your own bucket.
You were so happy and proud
when you learned to do things
on your own - like ride a bicycle,
read a book, or catch a ball.
You were filling your own bucket.

Filling your own bucket
is a big part of your happiness.

You fill at least TWO buckets whenever you are kind to others.

First, you fill their bucket by being thoughtful towards them.

Then, you fill your bucket because you feel happy when you help others feel happy.

Isn't it great to know that when you fill someone else's bucket, you fill your bucket, too?

The good feelings you give to others come back to you.

Filling a bucket is simple.

First, think of someone whose bucket you could fill.

Then, think of what you could do to fill it.

Could you invite a friend to join you for lunch?

13

Could you thank your mom or dad for a delicious dinner?

Could you take time
to play with your pet?
Even our pets have buckets!

15

Could you help
around the house?
Bucket filling is a terrific habit
because everyone is happier.

**Learning to fill buckets is
the first secret
to your happiness.**

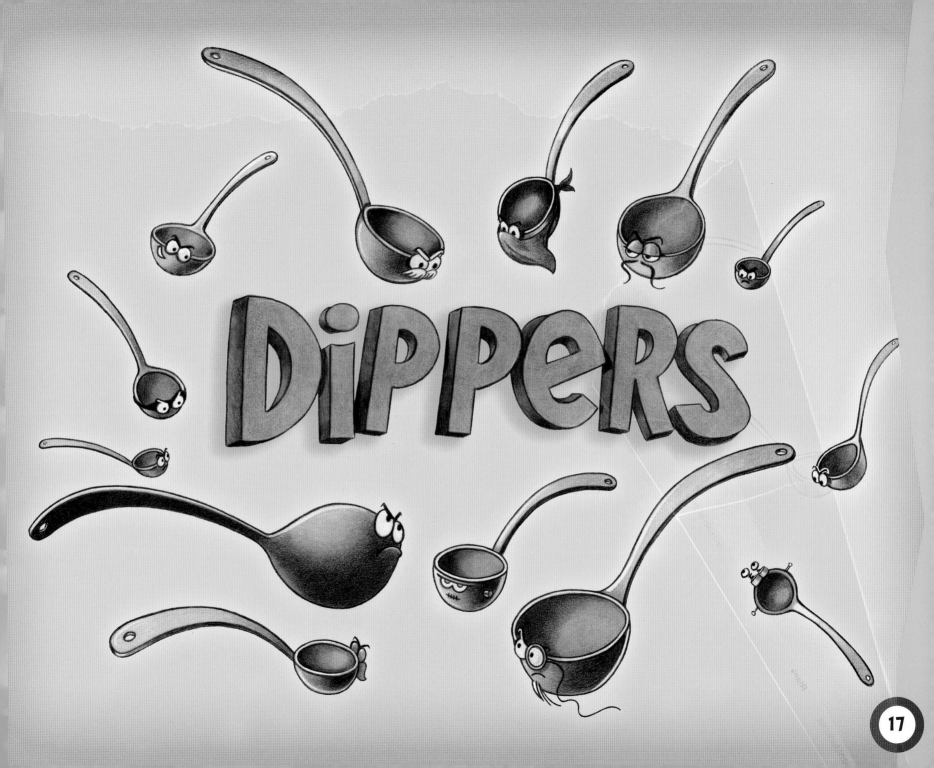

Dippers are what dip into buckets and remove some happiness.

Bucket dipping is the opposite of bucket filling. Instead of adding some good thoughts and feelings, bucket dipping takes some away. Bucket dipping is a terrible habit because no one is happier.

**There are many ways
to dip into buckets.**
Calling people names, bullying them, or
pointing and laughing at them
are just a few.
This is a mystery . . .
Why does everyone, including you, have
an invisible dipper?
And why would anyone have or use
something that takes happiness away?
No one knows for sure.

Bucket dipping could be a bad habit
that you learned from others.

You may think it's okay
to dip buckets if others do it.
Bucket dipping is not okay!

It is possible you don't know
that you're bucket dipping.
After all, buckets and dippers
are invisible. You can't see the actual
dipping, but . . .

When your bucket is
dipped, you will feel it.

Your dipper can have a mind of its own.
Unless you resist, it will jump into bucketdipping action before you know it,
especially if someone dips into your bucket first.

For example: What if your brother takes or breaks something special
that belongs to you? Quick as a blink, without thinking about it,
your dipper starts moving and then, watch out, you dip right back.
You might say things like, "Get lost!" or even, "I hate you."
You don't mean those things but . . .

When you let angry feelings become hurtful words,
your dipper takes a giant dip out of someone's bucket.

And what happens when you dip into buckets?
You don't fill your bucket. You empty it more.
You're not proud of yourself. You're less proud.
Your dipper can't take someone else's happiness
and put it in your bucket.

Bucket dipping hurts everyone.

Many people who dip into buckets will say the first thing that comes to mind. They haven't learned how to resist the urge to dip.

Everyone must learn not to dip because everyone has a dipper.

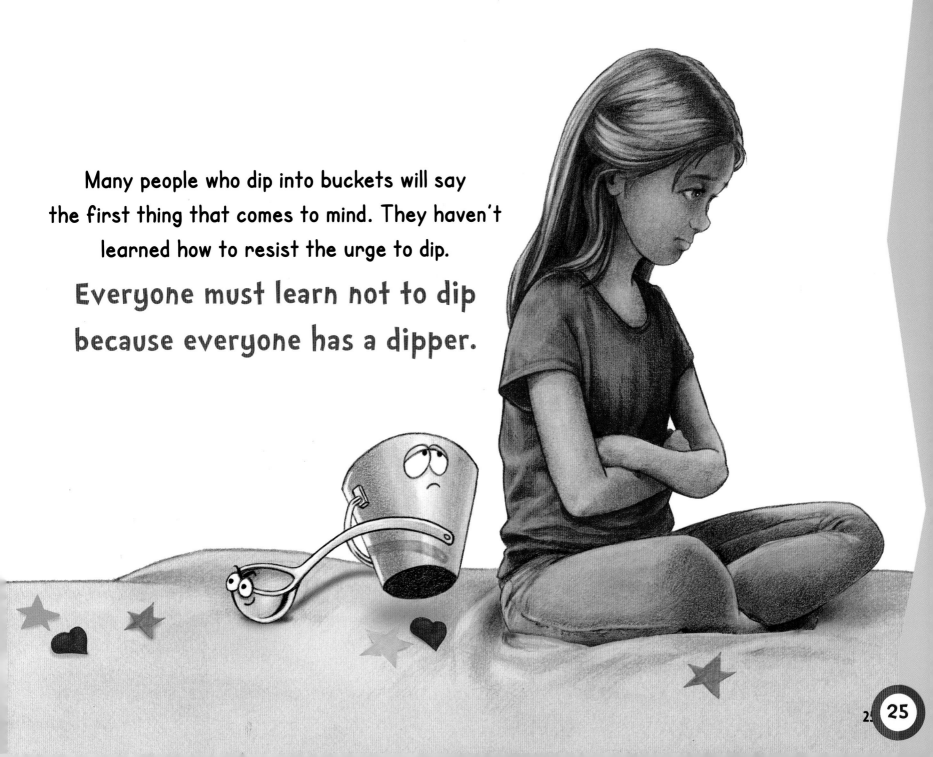

To keep everyone's bucket full, here are two good rules to follow:

1. Stop and think before you say anything.

2. If you can't say something nice,
   don't say anything at all.

Learning to resist the
urge to dip is the second
secret to your happiness.

You might be wondering . . . "What's a lid?"

Good question. Even many grown-ups don't know they have a lid.
And if you don't know you have a lid,
how will you keep your bucket from being dipped and emptied?
It will certainly get dipped at sometime, someday,
somewhere by someone.

Your lid helps protect the happiness in your bucket.

Do you know that you could be a super-great bucket filler who almost never dips,
and your bucket could be empty? How could that be?
It's because you don't know about your lid or how to use it.

Think of your bucket as being filled with precious jewels.
Do you want others to steal your treasures? No way!
Your happiness is just as valuable and you must protect it.
After all, your bucket holds your good thoughts and feelings
and you need to keep them.

That's why your bucket needs a lid.

Here is how your lid works . . .
When someone says or does something
that dips into your bucket, you feel it.
Instantly, you're not as happy as you were a minute ago.

You might feel sad, angry, hurt, scared or embarrassed.
Any "ouch" feeling is an important sign
warning you to . . . "Use your lid!"

Let's imagine someone rudely says to you,
"Where did you get that jacket?"

That "ouch" feeling is a sign your bucket
is getting dipped. It's time to use your lid.
Your lid says, "STOP!"
So, stop, take a deep breath, and think.
Don't dip back.

Remember . . .
This is your bucket and you
want it to stay full.

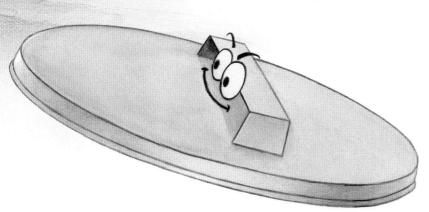

Your lid gives you time to stop and think.
It keeps you from losing more happiness
while you try to understand why someone is dipping.
Is this a bad habit they learned? Are they showing off?
In a hurry? Is their bucket a little low?

You can be sure that if someone says
or does something to hurt you, it is not about you.
It's about them and their bucket that is not full!

However, if you don't know the problem is their less-than-full bucket
and you dip back or remain hurt or angry, how will your bucket stay full?
Talk to people who know about bucket filling and I'm sure they'll agree.

There is another time when you may need your lid.

Do you know you can dip into your own bucket and take away your own happiness by what you tell yourself?

Yes, you can. One way you do this is by comparing yourself to others. For example: What if you're upset or jealous because your new baby brother or sister is getting more attention than you?

Use your lid to stop, think, and try to understand that people shine at different times and in different ways.

Remind yourself that every person is valuable and every person is a star, including you!
Your time to shine will come (even if it doesn't feel like it right now).

And do you know that the people who love you and you love the most
can dip into your bucket? And you can dip into theirs?

Bucket dipping happens in all families.

No one is perfect. Your lid helps you to understand, forgive, and protect the good
thoughts and feelings in your bucket.

But . . . Don't keep your lid on your bucket all the time.

If you do, how can people fill it? You only need your lid when someone is dipping. Most people—including parents, teachers, and friends—are awesome bucket fillers. And most of the time, they help to make your life terrific.

Here's one more good thing to know . . .
Your lid can help others and their lid can help you.
You do this when you stand up for one another.
However, if no one is around and your bucket is getting dipped,
you need to use your own lid to protect your own bucket or get help from others.

Learning to use your lid is the third secret to your happiness.

Now you know about invisible buckets, dippers, and lids and how they work.

First, everyone has a bucket and you can fill it with happiness.

And when you fill others', you fill your own bucket, too.
Do your best every day to be kind and treat everyone in the same
wonderful way that you would like to be treated.

Second, everyone has a dipper that can take happiness away.

You know that bucket dipping hurts everyone.

Do your best to resist the urge to dip.

And, if you slip and dip, be sure to admit your mistake and say you're sorry.

45

Third, everyone has a lid and lids protect happiness.

When someone is dipping, do your best to imagine their less-than-full bucket.

Maybe then you can understand and forgive them.

But if you need help, always go to another bucket filler.

Learning anything new, including these secrets
to your happiness, requires practice.

It can be difficult and you will make mistakes. Mistakes are a big part of learning, so don't give up. You can do it and it's worth the time and effort.

With practice, you will get better, you will be happier,

and you will help others be happier, too.

Now, it's up to you!

All around the world, thousands of people of all ages have taken the Bucket Filler's Pledge. We encourage you to make this same promise to yourself.

Bucket Fillers Pledge

I promise to do my best every day
to be a bucket filler, not to dip,
and to use my lid for myself and others
at home, at school, and everywhere I go.

About the Author

Carol McCloud is the author of ten books, which began with the ever-popular *Have You Filled a Bucket Today? A Guide to Daily Happiness for Kids* in 2006. Her books have sold three million copies and have been translated into more than a dozen languages. A champion for bucket filling, Carol strives to help people of all ages lead happier lives by growing in kindness, self-management, resilience, and compassion. She lives in Venice, Florida, with her husband, Jack. For information on books and sessions, visit cardinalrulepress.com.

About the Illustrator

Glenn Zimmer has been illustrating and designing books on bucket filling since 2013. Glenn is a seasoned art director and editorial illustrator. A graduate of the Art Institute of Philadelphia, Glenn currently serves on the faculty of Moore College of Art & Design in Pennsylvania. For more information, visit glennzimmer.com.